T0193451

Goodnight Christmas

by Fr. José Lucero, SDB

Illustrations by Fr. John Roche, SDB

Archway Publishing books may be ordered through booksellers or by contacting:

Archway Publishing
1663 Liberty Drive
Bloomington, IN 47403
www.archwaypublishing.com
844-669-3957

Scripture quotations taken from The Holy Bible, New International Version® NIV® Copyright © 1973 1978 1984 2011 by Biblica, Inc. TM. Used by permission. All rights reserved worldwide.

Interior Image Credit: Fr. John Roche, SDB

ISBN: 978-1-6657-2777-8 (sc)
ISBN: 978-1-6657-2776-1 (e)

Print information available on the last page.

Archway Publishing rev. date: 10/06/2022

Introduction

Christmas is a special time!
It is a time of warm and comforting lights,
a time of family and song, a time of cozy
houses and cozy teas, of dreaming and
tossing and turning waiting for the dawn.
Christmas is a time when heaven touches
the earth, when children listen for special
whispers and Moms and Dads hold onto
their hopes and their families, and their
faith, and their love for their God and
their lives.
Christmas is a special time! Make sure
you watch, listen, celebrate, and embrace
for Heaven has arrived.

Good night lights

Good night Christmas tree

Goodnight Bear

Good night family everywhere

Good night Kitchen

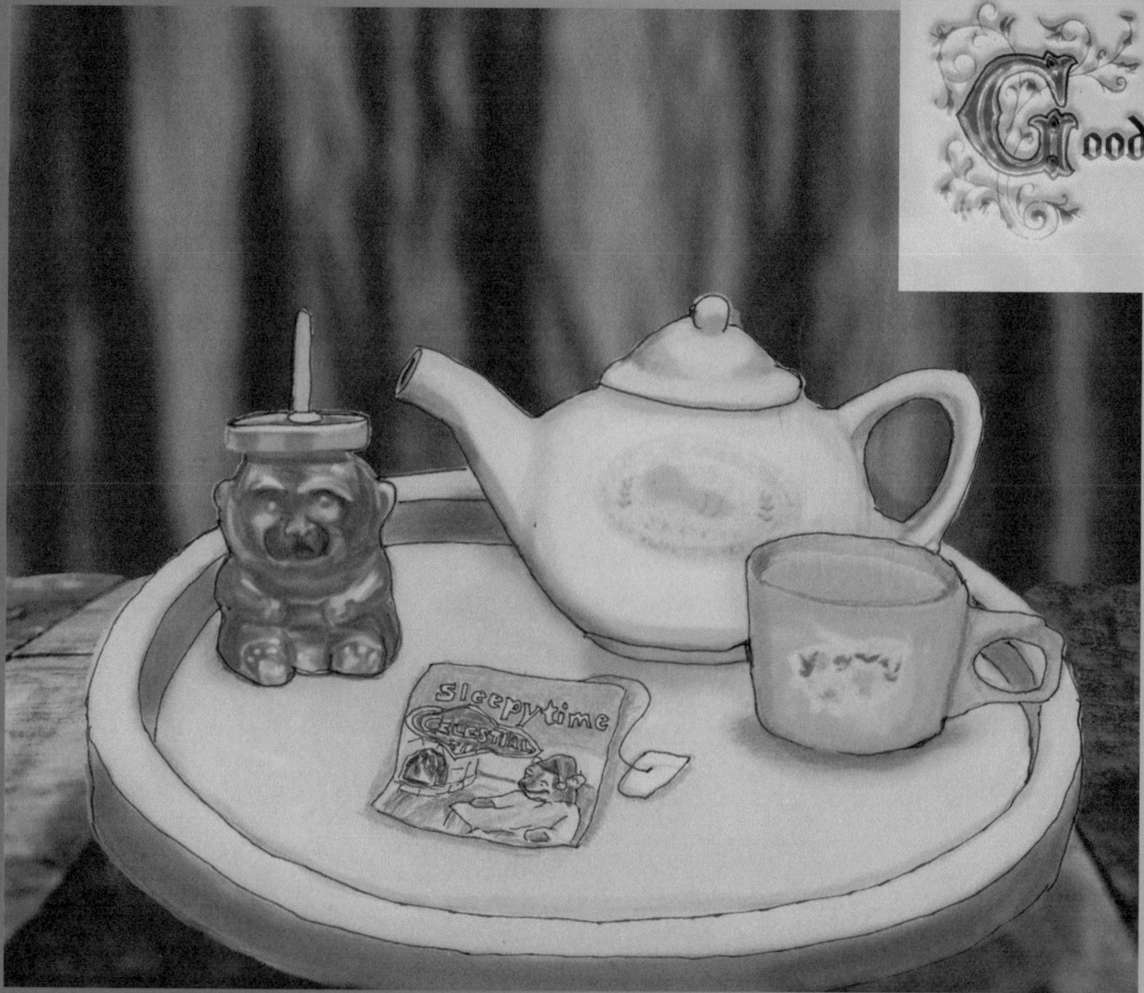
Sleepytime
CELESTIAL
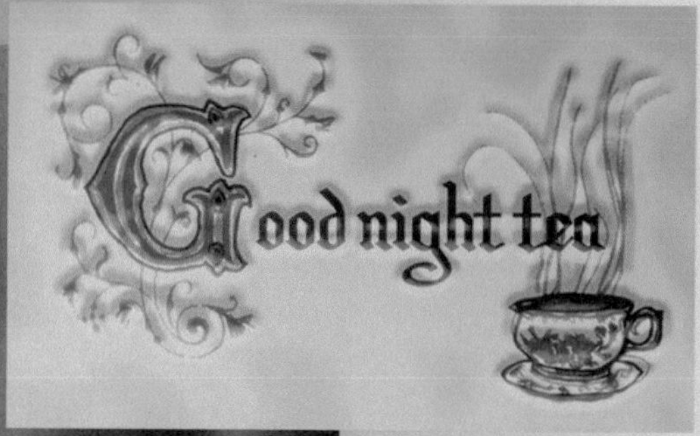
Goodnight tea

Good night cozy house

 Good night you and me

 hat dreams may come

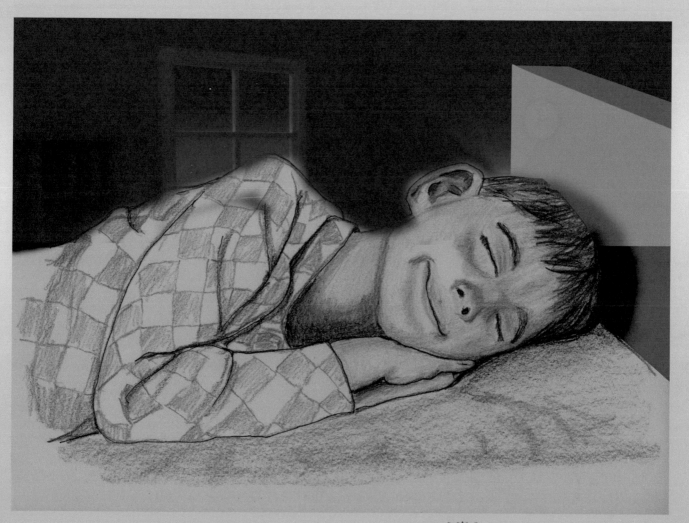

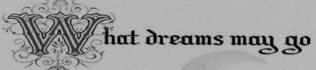

What dreams may go

Sleeping silently

My breath will flow

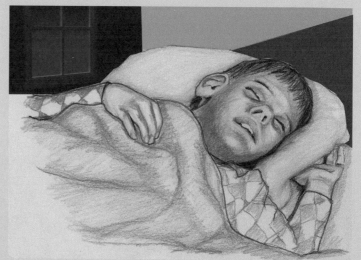

Tossing and turning

Idle and piddle

My body moves just a little

Alarms go off

 ut snooze insisting

Relaxation over

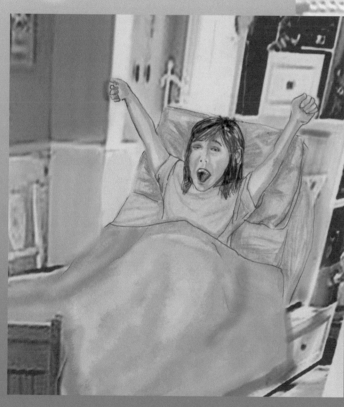

23

Awake resisting

Soft light flows

The tree glows

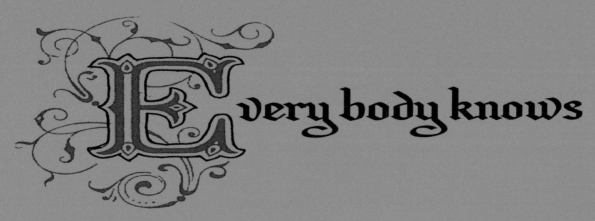

Every body knows

It's time for listening

Leading their thoughts to Heaven. . . .

This is not your typical Christmas book! This captures the simple yet profound memories of growing up on a ranch in New Mexico with a huge and sprawling family. Life was, and still is, filled with music and laughter and singing and so much more. Fr. Jose Lucero grew up in this special and blessed family and in a few lines captures the most treasured memories of Christmas Eve and Christmas morning. This is not about Santa Claus and reindeer, this is not even about presents. This is about PRESENCE and joy with one another. That, in the end, is the essence of the miracle of Incarnation. Our God is with us and promises to give us life and that to the full (John 10:10)!

Fr. John has been sketching and drawing since he can remember walking. As the long stretches of time came into the world with the Covid-19 pandemic, Fr. Jose reached out to his Salesian brother and friend, John, and challenged him to put his craft to work again. John was both delighted and challenged. From April 2020 to mid-July 2020, John drew, researched, learned new techniques and threw away about as many images as those found in this memoir of Fr. Jose. Fr. Jose and Fr. John hope that this simple sharing moves your heart and helps you find healing and joy as we move ahead in life.

Printed in the United States
by Baker & Taylor Publisher Services